F
CONTINUALLY AND...
WITH GOD

"Let nothing hinder thee from praying always . . ."
—Ecclesiasticus 18:22

St. Alphonsus Liguori
(1696-1787)
Bishop, Confessor, Doctor of the Church,
Founder of the Redemptorists

HOW TO CONVERSE
CONTINUALLY AND FAMILIARLY
WITH GOD

By

St. Alphonsus de Liguori

Translated by
Fr. L. X. Aubin, C.SS.R.

"Pray without ceasing."
—1 Thessalonians 5:17

TAN BOOKS AND PUBLISHERS, INC.
Rockford, Illinois 61105

Imprimi Potest: E. Chouinard

Nihil Obstat: L. Laplante, C.SS.R.
                    Provincial Superior
                    Ste-Anne de Beaupre

Imprimatur: ✠ J. M. R. Card. Villeneuve, OM.I.
                    Archbishop of Quebec

Published by the Daughters of St. Paul, Boston, circa 1963. Retypeset and published in 2005 by TAN Books and Publishers, Inc. with permission of the Redemptorist Fathers of Sainte-Anne-de-Beaupré (Quebec). Bible quotations have been converted to the Douay-Rheims version.

ISBN 0-89555-797-5

Cover illustration: Detail (one of the 12 Apostles) from "Assumption of Our Lady" stained-glass window. Photo copyright © 1992 by Alan Brown. Used by arrangement with Al Brown Photo, 3597 N. Roberts Rd., Bardstown, KY 40004.

Printed and bound in the United States of America.

TAN BOOKS AND PUBLISHERS, INC.
P.O. Box 424
Rockford, Illinois 61105

2005

"Acquire the habit of speaking to God
as if you were alone with Him,
familiarly and with confidence and love,
as to the dearest and most loving of friends.
Speak to Him often of your business,
your plans, your troubles, your fears—
of everything that concerns you.
Converse with Him confidently and frankly;
for God is not wont to speak to a soul
that does not speak to Him."

—St. Alphonsus de Liguori

Contents

HOW TO CONVERSE
CONTINUALLY AND FAMILIARLY
WITH GOD

"Pray, lest ye enter into temptation."
—Luke 22:40

∽ Chapter 1 ∽

Love and Confidence

JOB was astonished at seeing Almighty God so intent on doing good to us that He seems to have nothing more at heart than to love us and to induce us to love Him in return. In his amazement he cried out to the Lord: *"What is man that Thou art mindful of him? or the son of man that Thou visitest him?"* (Ps. 8:5). Is it not a mistake, then, to think it a lack of respect for God's infinite Majesty to act toward Him with great confidence and familiarity?

Assuredly, Loving Souls, you should go to God with all humility and respect, humbling yourselves in His presence, especially when you remember your past ingratitude and sins. Yet you should practice the greatest possible love and confidence in treating with Him. True, He is infinite Majesty, but He is also infinite

1

Goodness and infinite Love. There can be no greater Lord than God; neither can there be a more ardent lover than He. Far from despising our confidence in Him, He rejoices that we have it—confidence and familiarity and affection like that which little children show toward their mothers.

Behold how He invites us to come to Him, and the loving embraces which He promises to lavish on us: *"You shall be carried at the breasts, and upon the knees they shall caress you. As one whom the mother caresseth, so will I comfort you."* (*Is.* 66:12-13). Just as a mother finds pleasure in taking her little child on her lap, there to feed and caress him, in like manner our loving God shows His fondness for His beloved souls who have given themselves entirely to Him and have placed all their hope in His goodness.

∽ Chapter 2 ∾

Why Have You Loved Me?

CONSIDER that no one—whether friend or brother, father or mother, lover or spouse—loves you more than your God. And divine grace is the inestimable treasure through which vile creatures and servants like ourselves become dear friends of our Creator. *"For she is an infinite treasure to men! which they that use, become the friends of God."* (*Wis.* 7:14). It was for the purpose of increasing our confidence that He *"emptied Himself"* (*Phil.* 2:7), so to speak, humbling Himself to the point of becoming a man in order to live in familiar converse with us. *"He conversed with men."* (*Bar.* 3:38). He went so far as to become a little Babe and to live in poverty and die on a cross for our sake. He even placed Himself under the species of bread so as to be with us always and in the most intimate union. *"He that eateth My Flesh, and drinketh My Blood, abideth in Me, and I in him."* (*John* 6:57).

In short, so great is God's love for you that He seems to love no one but you. And therefore, you should love no one but Him.* You should be able to say to Him: *"My Beloved to me, and I to Him."* (*Cant.* 2:16). My God has given Himself entirely to me, and I give my whole self to Him; He has chosen me for His beloved, and I choose Him from among all for my only love. *"My Beloved is white and ruddy, chosen out of thousands."* (*Cant.* 5:10).

Often, therefore, speak to God in these words: "O my Lord, why have You loved me so much? What good do You find in my poor self? Have You forgotten the injuries I have done You? But since You have treated me with so much love—for instead of condemning me to Hell, You have given me graces without number— I will henceforth love no one but You, my

---

*That is, we should love only God with an *absolute* love which supersedes every other consideration.
—*Publisher*, 2005.

God and my all. What grieves me most in my past offenses, O my loving God, is not so much the punishment I have deserved, as the displeasure I have given You, Who are worthy of infinite love. But You never reject a repentant and humble heart. *'A contrite and humbled heart, O God, Thou wilt not despise.'* (*Ps.* 50:19). Now indeed I wish for no one else but You alone in this life and in the next. *'For what have I in Heaven? and besides Thee what do I desire upon earth? . . . Thou art the God of my heart, and the God that is my portion forever.'* (*Ps.* 72:25-26). You alone are and will always be the only Lord of my heart and will; You alone my only good, my heaven, my hope, my all. *'Thou art the God of my heart, and the God that is my portion forever.'"* (*Ps.* 72:26).

∽ Chapter 3 ∽

The Mercies of the Lord

IF you wish to strengthen your confidence in God still more, often recall the loving way in which He has acted toward you, and how mercifully He has tried to bring you out of your sinful life, to break your attachment to the things of earth and draw you to His love. With such thoughts in your mind, now that you have resolved to love Him and please Him with all your strength, your only fear should be to fear God too much and to place too little confidence in Him. There can be no surer pledge of His love for you than His past mercies toward you. God is displeased at the diffidence of souls who love Him sincerely and whom He Himself loves. If, therefore, you wish to please His loving heart, go to Him henceforth with the greatest possible confidence and affection.

"Behold, I have graven thee in My hands: thy walls are always before My eyes." (Is. 49:16). "Beloved Soul," says the Lord, "why do you fear? Why are you afraid? Your name is written in My hands so that I may never forget to do you good. Perhaps you are afraid of your enemies? Know that I can never forget to protect you, since I have always before My eyes the charge of your defense." With this thought to rejoice him, David said to God: *"O Lord, Thou hast crowned us, as with a shield of Thy good will."* (Ps. 5:13). Who, O Lord, can ever do us harm if Your loving kindness is cast all around us as a wall of defense?

Above all, reanimate your confidence by thinking of the gift which God has given us in the person of Jesus Christ. *"God so loved the world, as to give His only-begotten Son."* (John 3:16). How can we fear, asks the Apostle, that God will ever deny us anything since He has given us His own Son? *"He that spared not even His own Son, but delivered Him up for us all, how hath He not also, with Him, given us all things?"* (Rom. 8:32).

Chapter 4

The Paradise of God

"**M**Y *delights were to be with the children of men.*" (Prov. 8:31). The heart of man is, so to speak, the paradise of God. Oh, love the God who loves you! Since His delights are to be with you, let yours be found in Him. Spend all the days of your life with Him in whose company you hope to pass an eternity of bliss.

Acquire the habit of speaking to God as if you were alone with Him, familiarly and with confidence and love, as to the dearest and most loving of friends. It is a great mistake, as we have already remarked, to be afraid of Him and to act in His presence like a timid and craven slave trembling with fright before his master. But a far greater mistake it would be to think that to converse with God is wearisome and bitter. No, it cannot be. *"For her conversation hath no bitterness, nor her company any tediousness, but joy and gladness."* (*Wis.* 8:16).* Ask those who love Him with a sincere love, and they will tell you that they find no greater or prompter relief amid the troubles of their life than in loving conversation with their Divine Friend.

You are not asked to apply your mind continually to the thought of God and lay aside the fulfillment of your duties and your recreations. Nothing else is required than to act toward God, in the midst of your occupations, as you do, even when busy, toward those who love you and whom you love.

Your God is ever beside you—indeed, He is even within you. *"In Him we live, and move, and are."* (*Acts* 17:28). Not only is there no need of an intermediary through whom He would want you to speak to Him, but He finds His delight in having you treat with Him personally and in all confidence. Speak to Him often

---

*In the Old Testament book of *Wisdom*, God's attribute of divine Wisdom is personified as *she*.
                                        —*Publisher*, 2005.

of your business, your plans, your troubles, your fears—of everything that concerns you. But above all, converse with Him confidently and frankly; for God is not wont to speak to a soul that does not speak to Him.

∾ Chapter 5 ∾

"Taste and See . . ."

IF a soul is a stranger to God's conversation, she will hardly hear His voice when He speaks to her, as He Himself complains: *"Our sister is little . . . What shall we do to our sister in the day when she is to be spoken to?"* (*Cant.* 8:8). Our sister is like a little child in My love: How can I speak to her if she does not understand what I say? God wishes to be feared as a mighty and terrible Lord by those who despise His grace; but on the other hand, He wishes to be treated like a most affectionate friend by those who love Him. Hence, He desires that we speak to Him often with familiarity and without any restriction.

True, the greatest reverence is due to God; but if He gives you the grace of feeling His presence and the desire to speak to Him as to the one who loves you more than anyone else, tell Him your thoughts freely and confidently. *"Wisdom . . . is easily seen by them that love her, and is found by them that seek her."* (Wis. 6:13). When you desire His love, He does not wait until you go to Him, but He anticipates you and comes to you Himself with the graces and remedies you need. He only waits for you to speak to Him, in order to prove that He is near at hand, ready to hear and comfort you. *"In my affliction I called upon the Lord . . . and my cry before Him came into His ears."* (Ps. 17:7).

God is everywhere by His immensity; but He has fixed a special abode in two places: in Heaven, where He is present by the glory He imparts to the Blessed; and on earth, in the humble soul that loves Him: *"The Lord is nigh unto them that are of a contrite heart: and He will save the humble of spirit."* (Ps. 33:19). Although our God dwells in the highest Heaven, still He does not disdain to treat with His faithful servants day and night in their grottoes or in their cells. There He bestows on them His divine consolations, a single one of which far exceeds all worldly delights—consolations which can be appreciated only by one who has experienced them. *"O taste and see that the Lord is sweet . . ."* (*Ps.* 33:9).

∽ Chapter 6 ∽

Every Moment of Every Hour

FRIENDS in the world have their hours of conversation together, but they also have hours of separation. Such is not the case, however, with God and you; if you but wish, there will never be any separation from Him: *"If thou sleep, thou shalt not fear: thou shalt rest, and thy sleep shall be sweet . . . For the Lord will be at thy side."* (Prov. 3:24, 26). God will be beside you when you sleep, always keeping watch over you: *"When I go into my house, I shall repose myself with her: for her conversation hath no bitterness, nor her company any tediousness."* (Wis. 8:16). He does not go away from your bedside when you rest. Rather, He continues to think of you always, so that if you awake during the night, He may speak to you by His inspirations and receive in return from you an act of love or of oblation or of thanksgiving; and in this way, even during the night, He keeps up His loving conversation with you. Sometimes He even speaks to you in your sleep and makes His voice sound in your ears, that you may put His wishes into execution when you awake. *"I will speak to him in a dream."* (*Num.* 12:6).

And again in the morning, He is there waiting to hear some acts of love and confidence from you and to treasure your waking thoughts and the work you promise to do for Him during the day, as well as the sufferings you will patiently bear for His glory and love. Now just as He is sure to be present with you at the very moment you awake, even so, do not fail on your part to cast a loving glance at Him and rejoice at hearing from your God Himself the glad news that He is not far from you as He was in times past because of your sins. He loves you and wishes to be loved by you, and hence when you awake, He lovingly intimates to you His commandment: *"Thou shalt love the Lord thy God with thy whole heart."* (*Matt.* 22:37).

❦ Chapter 7 ❦

Love Will Find Words

YOU ought therefore never to forget God's presence, as most men do. Speak to Him as often as you can, for it does not tire Him, nor does He hold it in contempt, as do great men of the world. If you love Him, you will always have something to say to Him. Tell Him whatever comes to your mind about yourself and your affairs, as you would tell an intimate friend. Do not look upon Him as a high and mighty lord who desires to speak only to great ones—and then, only of great things. Our God delights in stooping down to converse with us, and He rejoices when we make known to Him our most trivial everyday affairs.

Such is His love and care for you that He seems to have no one else but you of whom to think. He is so concerned with

17

your interests that He seems to have no providence except to preserve you, no almighty power except to help you, no mercy or kindness except to have compassion on you, to do you good and win you to His love and confidence by His kind attention.

Then freely open your heart to Him and ask Him to lead you to do His Divine Will in a perfect manner. Let all your designs and desires be directed only toward knowing His good pleasure and gratifying His Divine Heart. *"Bless God at all times, and desire of Him to direct thy ways, and that all thy counsels may abide in Him."* (*Tob.* 4:20).

Do not say: "But why should I make known to God all my needs, since He sees and knows them better than I?" Surely He does, but He acts as if He were not aware of the wants which you neglect to disclose to Him and for which you do not ask His divine help. Our Saviour knew very well that Lazarus was dead; yet He did not reveal the fact that He knew it until Magdalen told Him, and then He consoled her by raising her brother to life.

When, therefore, you are suffering from some sickness, temptation, persecution or other trouble, go to Him at once and ask Him to reach out to you His helping hand. No sooner will you have put before His eyes your affliction by saying: *"Behold, O Lord, for I am in distress . . ."* (*Lam.* 1:20), than He will console you, or at least give you strength to suffer patiently the passing trial, and it will have been better for you to have had that trial than to have been delivered from it. Make known to God all feelings of sadness or fear that oppress you, and say to Him: "O my God, all my hopes are in You. I offer You this affliction and conform myself to Your Will. But have pity on me, and either deliver me from it or give me strength to suffer it." And God will surely fulfill in you the promise He made in the Gospel always to console and comfort the afflicted when they have recourse to Him: *"Come to Me, all you that labour, and are burdened, and I will refresh you."* (*Matt.* 11:28).

∽ Chapter 8 ∽

Source of All Consolation

GOD will not be displeased if you seek consolation from your friends; still, He wishes that principal recourse be had to Him. At least, after you have in vain sought solace from creatures, come to your Creator and say to Him: "Men, O Lord, have nothing but words for me: *'and my familiar friends also are departed from me.'* (*Job* 6:13). They cannot raise my low spirits; I will never again seek consolation from them. You are all my hope and all my love: from You alone do I look for comfort—and my comfort will be to do what pleases You most on this occasion. I am ready to bear this cross during my whole life and for all eternity, if such be Your good pleasure. Only help me."

Do not be afraid that you will displease Him if you at times quietly complain to

Him and say: *"Why, O Lord, hast Thou retired afar off?"* (*Ps.* 9:1). "You know that I love You and long for nothing else than Your love. Take pity on me and help me, do not forsake me." If your anguish does not diminish but instead continues to bother you, then unite your prayers to those of Jesus Christ dying in utter desolation on the Cross, and cry out to Him for mercy, saying: *"My God, my God, why hast Thou forsaken me?"* (*Matt.* 27:46).

This trial should serve but to increase your humility at the thought that one who has offended God does not deserve consolation; and it should occasion a renewal of your confidence in Him, in knowing that God does or permits everything only for your good: *"And we know that to them that love God, all things work together unto good."* (*Rom.* 8:28). The more weary and discouraged you may feel, the more confidently should you cry out: *"The Lord is my light and my salvation, whom shall I fear?"* (*Ps.* 26:1). "You, O Lord, must enlighten me, You must save me. I trust in You." *"In Thee, O my God, I put my trust; let me not be ashamed."* (*Ps.* 24:2). Prayers such as these should restore peace to your soul, for no one has ever been lost who has placed his hopes in Him. *"For none of them that wait on Thee shall be confounded."* (*Ps.* 24:3).

~ Chapter 9 ~

The God of Salvation

CONSIDER that your God loves you more than you can possibly love Him. What do you fear? David found comfort in these words: *"The Lord hath been mindful of us . . ."* (Ps. 113:12). Then you should say to Him: "Into Your arms I cast myself, O my God. I want to think of nothing but of loving You and giving You pleasure. Behold I am ready to do whatever You shall ask of me. Not only do You desire my welfare; You are solicitous for it. Therefore, I leave to You the care of my salvation. In You is my rest, and it will always be in You, since You will that I place all my hopes in You. *'In peace in the selfsame I will sleep, and I will rest: For Thou, O Lord, singularly hast settled me in hope.'"* (Ps. 4:9-10).

"Think of the Lord in goodness." (Wis. 1:1). The wise man exhorts us by these

words to have greater confidence in the divine mercy than fear of the divine justice, since God is far more inclined to do good than to chastise. So says St. James: *"Mercy exalteth itself above judgment."* (*Jas.* 2:13). Hence the Apostle St. Peter warns us that in the fears we feel for our concerns, be they temporal or eternal, we must abandon ourselves entirely to the good God, who has our salvation so much at heart: *"Casting all your care upon Him, for He hath care of you."* (*1 Ptr.* 5:7). In this same regard, how beautiful is the title which David gives the Lord when he says that our God is the God who seeks to save: *"For He is my God and my Saviour . . ."* (*Ps.* 61:7). This means, according to [St. Robert] Cardinal Bellarmine, that God's own particular office is, not to condemn, but to save everyone; for even though He threatens with His disfavor those who despise Him, His mercy is assured to those who fear Him, as our Blessed Mother sang in her *Magnificat:* *"And His mercy is from generation unto generations, to them that fear Him."* (*Luke* 1:50).

These texts of Scripture I set before you, O Devout Soul, in order that, when you are troubled by the thought whether you will be saved or lost, whether you are predestined or not, you may relieve your mind by considering the desire God has to save you, as is proved by His promises, if only you stand firm in your resolution to serve and love Him as He demands.

∽ Chapter 10 ∽

Rejoice in the Lord

WHEN you receive some pleasant news, do not act as certain unfaithful and ungrateful persons are wont to do: They pray to God in adversity but forget and abandon Him in prosperity. Be as faithful to Him as you are to a friend who loves you and desires your welfare. Go at once to God and tell Him of your joy; praise and thank Him for it, and thus acknowledge that it is entirely a gift from His bounty. And rejoice in this happiness because it has been bestowed upon you by His good pleasure. In Him alone, therefore, seek joy and consolation: *"My soul shall rejoice in the Lord; and shall be delighted in His salvation."* (Ps. 34:9). Say to Him: "My Jesus, I bless You and will always bless You for the many graces bestowed on me when I deserve not graces but chastisements because of my many offenses against You." Say to Him with the Sacred Spouse: *"'In our gates are all fruits: the new and the old, my Beloved, I have kept for Thee.'* (*Cant.* 7:13). I thank You, O Lord; I wish to be mindful of Your benefits, both past and present, in order to render You honor and glory for them forever."

But if you love God, you should rejoice more in His happiness than in your own. One who has a very dear friend sometimes feels happier over his friend's good than over his own personal welfare. Then take comfort in the thought that your God is infinitely blessed. Say to Him often: "My beloved Lord, I rejoice more in Your happiness than in any good thing I have; indeed I do, because I love You more than I love myself."

Another mark of confidence which greatly gratifies your loving God is to cast yourself at once at His feet and ask pardon when you commit some fault. Consider that God is so inclined to forgive sinners that He weeps over their loss when they stray far from Him and live in a state of spiritual death. He lovingly calls them in these words: *"Why will you die, O house of Israel? . . . Return ye and live."* (*Ezech.* 18:31-32). He promises to welcome the sinner who has abandoned Him as soon as he returns to His arms: *"Return to Me, and I will return to you, saith the Lord of hosts."* (*Mal.* 3:7). Oh, would that sinners knew with what tenderness the Lord is waiting for them to grant them pardon! *"Therefore the Lord waiteth that He may have mercy on you . . . He will surely have pity on thee . . ."* (*Is.* 30:18-19). If only they realized the desire He has not to chastise them but to see them converted, to embrace them and press them to His Heart. He makes this solemn declaration: *"I desire not the death of the wicked, but that the wicked turn from his way and live."* (*Ezech.* 33:11). He goes so far as to say: *"If your sins be as scarlet, they shall be made as white as snow."* (*Is.* 1:18). In other words: "Sinners, repent of having offended Me and then come to Me, and if I do not forgive you, accuse Me, blame Me, and treat Me as one who has broken his promise.

But I will stand by My promise. If you come to Me, rest assured that, even though your conscience be black, My grace will make it white as snow."

❧ Chapter 11 ❧

"A Contrite and Humble Heart"

FINALLY, God has declared that when a person repents of having offended Him, He forgets all his sins: *"And their sins and iniquities I will remember no more."* (*Heb.* 10:17). So whenever you fall into some sin, raise your eyes at once to God, make an act of love and, while acknowledging your sin, confidently hope for pardon and say to Him: *"'Lord, he whom Thou lovest is sick'* (*John* 11:3); the heart which You love is sick and covered with sores: *'O Lord . . . heal my soul, for I have sinned against Thee.'"* (*Ps.* 40:5). Say: "You go about seeking repentant sinners: behold one of them at Your feet, seeking You. The evil is done: what am I to do? You will not have me lose heart. Even though I have sinned, You wish me well, and I am sorry for the displeasure I have caused You. I propose not to do it again. You who are that God *'who is gracious and merciful: patient and plenteous in mercy' (Ps.* 144:8), forgive me. Let me hear the words You once spoke to Magdalen: *'Thy sins are forgiven thee' (Luke* 7:48), and give me strength to be faithful in the future."

But particularly when you have fallen into sin, cast a glance at Jesus on the Cross so that you may not be discouraged; offer His merits to the Eternal Father, and then firmly hope for pardon, since, in order to forgive you, He has *"spared not even His own Son . . ." (Rom.* 8:32). Say to Him full of confidence: *"Look on the face of Thy Christ." (Ps.* 83:10). "O my God, look on Your Son who died for me; and through love of Him, forgive me."

Reflect attentively, O Devout Soul, on the teaching commonly given by spiritual masters: namely, that you should at once turn to God after you have been unfaithful to Him, even though it be the hundredth time in the day, and you should be at peace again after your faults and after recommending yourself to God, as has been said. Otherwise, if your soul remains discouraged and troubled by the sin you have committed, you will converse but little with God; your confidence in Him will grow less; your desire to love Him will become cold; and you will make little progress in the way of the Lord. On the other hand, if you turn to God at once to ask His pardon and to promise amendment, your faults will help you to advance further in divine love. It is not a rare occurrence among intimate friends that their friendship is strengthened when one has displeased the other but has afterwards humbled himself and asked pardon. Do likewise: Let your sins serve to bind you more closely in love to your God.

∽ **Chapter 12** ∽

What Will You
Have Me Do, Lord?

WHEN you are troubled by any sort of doubt, whether it be caused by yourself or by others, act as do faithful friends who take counsel from each other about any matter that presents itself: Never fail to give God a proof of your confidence by asking His advice and praying to Him to enlighten you to resolve on what will be to His good pleasure. *"Put Thou words in my mouth, and strengthen the resolution in my heart."* (*Jdth.* 9:18). "Tell me, O Lord, what You wish me to do or to answer, and that will I do. *'Speak, Lord, for Thy servant heareth.'"* (*1 Kgs.* 3:9).

Again, prove to God your confidence by recommending to Him not only your personal needs, but also those of others. God is greatly pleased when, forgetful occa-

sionally of your own affairs, you speak to
Him about what concerns His glory, about
your neighbor's difficulties, especially
about those who are troubled and
afflicted, about the souls in Purgatory
who yearn to see Him, and about poor
sinners who are deprived of His grace.
For these latter in particular, say to God:
"O Lord, You are so lovable and worthy
of infinite love! How can You bear that
so many souls in this world, on whom
You lavish such great favors, refuse to
know and to love You? Nay, they even
offend and despise You. Ah, most loving
God, make Yourself known, make Yourself loved! *'Hallowed be Thy name, Thy
kingdom come!'* (*Matt.* 7:9-10). May Your
name be adored and loved by all men!
Let Your love rule supreme in all hearts!
I beseech You, let me not depart from You
without You granting me some grace for
those poor souls on whose behalf I am
praying to You."

∽ **Chapter 13** ∽

"After This Our Exile . . ."

IT is said that there is in Purgatory a special suffering, called the pain of languishing, for those souls who, while on earth, had little desire for Heaven. This is as it should be, for one shows small appreciation for the beautiful and eternal kingdom which Our Redeemer purchased for us by His death if he desires it but little. Therefore, Loving Souls, never forget to sigh often for Heaven, while saying to your God that it seems as if a thousand years separate you from the day on which you will see and love Him face to face. Develop a great longing to leave this land of exile, this place full of sin and fraught with danger of losing His divine grace: a great longing to come to that land of love where you will love Him with all your strength.

Often say to Him: "As long, O Lord, as

I live on this earth, I always run the risk
of wandering away from You and of losing Your love. When will the day come
on which I shall depart from this life
where I always offend You? When shall
I begin to love You with all my soul and
be united to You without fear of losing
You any more?" Such was the continual
desire of St. Teresa of Avila, to whom the
sound of the clock gave fresh joy at the
thought that another hour had been
struck off her life and the danger of losing God. So intense was her longing for
death, which would enable her to see God,
that she died from her desire of dying.
Therefore, she composed her hymn of
love: *"I die, because I do not die."*

Finally, if you wish to please the loving Heart of your God, try for as long a
space of time as you can to converse with
Him, with the greatest possible confidence; He will not fail to answer you and
even to speak with you Himself. Not that
He will make audible sounds strike your
ears, but He will answer in words that
you will clearly understand in your heart,
insofar as you leave conversation with

creatures and try to speak with your God—you alone with Him alone: *"I will lead her into the wilderness: and I will speak to her heart."* (*Osee* 2:14). Then will He speak to you with those inspirations, those interior lights, those manifestations of His goodness, those gentle knockings at the door of your heart, those pledges of pardon, those feelings of peace, that hope of Heaven, that interior joy, the delightful sweetness of His grace, the loving union and intimate contact with Him: in a word, He will speak to you with those words of love which are readily understood by the souls whom He loves and who seek nothing but Him.

∽ Chapter 14 ∽

Sanctify Every Day

FINALLY, in order to summarize briefly what is scattered throughout the previous pages, I wish to point out a devotional practice which will render all your daily actions pleasing to God. When you awake in the morning, your first thought should be to raise your mind to God and offer Him all the actions of that day, asking Him to help you by His grace. Then make the other morning Christian acts of thanksgiving, love, petition, and the firm resolve of living during that day as if it were the last day of your life. Father St.-Jure* teaches that one should, in the morning, make an agreement with the Divine Saviour:

---

*See *Trustful Surrender to Divine Providence*, by Fr. St.-Jure and St. Claude de la Colombiere. (TAN, 1983). —*Publisher*, 2005.

namely, that whenever you make certain signs, such as putting your hand on your heart, lifting your eyes heavenward or to the crucifix, or similar things, it is your intention to make an act of love, an act of desire to see Him loved by all, an act of self-offering, and the like.

After you have made the preceding acts, place your soul in the side of Jesus and under the mantle of Mary, and pray the Eternal Father, for the love of Jesus and Mary, to preserve you during the day. Then, before any other action, make at once at least half an hour of mental prayer or meditation; and the principal topic of your meditation should be the sufferings and contempt that our Blessed Lord endured in His Passion. This is the subject which is most precious to devout souls and which most inflames them with divine love.

There are three devotions which you must treasure above all the others if you want to grow in holiness: devotion to the Passion, to the Most Blessed Sacrament, and to the Blessed Virgin. In your meditations make frequent acts of contrition, love of God and self-oblation. The Venerable Father Charles Caraffa, founder of the *Pious Workers,* used to say that one fervent act of love in the morning meditation is sufficient to keep the soul fervent throughout the remainder of the day.

∽ Chapter 15 ∽

Every Action with God
And for God

ESPECIALLY, then, in your other acts of devotion, such as Confession, Communion, the Divine Office, etc., when engaged in external occupations such as study, manual labor, or the duties of your state of life, do not neglect, at the beginning of every action, to offer it to God and to ask for His help to perform it well. Acquire the habit of retiring often into the cell of your heart, there to be united with God, as St. Catherine of Siena was wont to do. In short, whatever you do, do it with God and for God.

When you leave your room or your house and when you return, recommend yourself to the Blessed Mother by saying a *Hail Mary*. When going to table for your meals, offer to God whatever pleasure or displeasure you may feel in eating or drinking; and after the meal, thank Him by saying: "What benefits, O Lord, You bestow on one who has so greatly offended You!" Sometime during the day, make spiritual reading and a visit to the Blessed Sacrament and to the Blessed Virgin;* and in the evening, recite the Rosary and make an examination of conscience together with the Christian Acts of Faith, Hope, Charity, Contrition and firm purpose of amendment, as well as resolutions to receive the Holy Sacraments during life and at the moment of your death, and to gain all the indulgences attached to these acts. Upon going to bed, reflect that you ought to be in the fire of Hell;** and go to sleep with the crucifix in your arms and with these

---

*See the book *Visits to the Blessed Sacrament and the Blessed Virgin Mary*, by St. Alphonsus Liguori (TAN, 2000). —*Publisher*, 2005.

**St. Alphonsus' meaning is that if a person has ever in his life committed a mortal sin—and this, unfortunately, would seem to be true of most persons—he has done an act that was deserv-

words on your lips: *"In peace in the selfsame I will sleep, and I will rest: For
Thou, O Lord, singularly hast settled me
in hope."* (Ps. 4:9-10).

---

ing of Hell, even if that sin were later forgiven
and its everlasting punishment remitted.
                              —*Publisher*, 2005.

∽ Chapter 16 ∽

Keep Eternity Near at Hand

IN order always to keep recollected and united with God in this life, insofar as possible, take advantage of all that you hear and see to raise your mind to God and to remind you of eternity. For example, when you look at water trickling from a leaking container, reflect that, in the same way, your life is ebbing away and death is drawing near. A lamp running low for want of oil should remind you that one day your life also will have to come to an end. At the sight of a funeral or of a corpse, remember that you also will have to die. If you see the great ones of this earth rejoicing in their dignity and wealth, have compassion on their folly and say: "God is enough for me." "*Some* trust *in chariots, and some in horses: but we will call upon the name of the Lord our God.*" (*Ps.* 19:8). "They rejoice in vain things: no other glory do I want but to be in God's grace and to love Him."

When you witness magnificent obsequies or see imposing monuments on the graves of famous men, say to yourself: "What does all this avail them if they are damned?" When you gaze at the sea, noting whether it be tranquil or stormy, behold in this the difference between a soul that is in God's grace and one that is not. A tree that has dried up should put you in mind of a soul deprived of God, good for nothing except to be burned. If you should ever see a culprit tremble with shame and fright before his judge or his father or superior because of some grave offense, imagine how frightened a sinner will be in the presence of Christ the Judge! At the rumbling of thunder and when you are afraid, think of the fear that shakes the damned on hearing constantly in Hell the thunders of the divine justice.

Chapter 17

Creation's Hymn of Praise

IF you ever happen to hear someone who has been condemned to death remark in his grief: "Is there then no escape from death for me?" consider in what state of despair will be the soul that is condemned to Hell and cries out: "Can nothing then prevent my eternal ruin?"

When you view fields and seashores, flowers and fruits, which gladden you with their appearance or with their fragrance, say: "How many beautiful things God has made for me on this earth in order that I may love Him! What further delights He has in store for me in Heaven!" St. Teresa of Avila, on seeing beautiful hills and landscapes, used to say that they reproached her for her ingratitude toward God. The Abbot de Rance, founder of the Trappist Order, was wont to remark that these wonderful things of created nature reminded him of the obligation to love God. St. Augustine said the same in these words: *"Heaven and earth and all things tell me to love You."* The story is told of a certain holy man who, while walking through the fields, would gently strike with a stick the flowers and plants he met on his way. *"Do not speak any more,"* he would say; *"do not reproach me with my ingratitude to God. I hear you; keep quiet; that is enough."* St. Mary Magdalen of Pazzi, when she held in her hand a fruit or flower, felt herself wounded by divine love. *"Behold,"* she would say, *"how my God has thought for all eternity of creating this fruit and this flower as a token of His love for me."*

∽ Chapter 18 ∾

God Your Only Good

WHEN you look at rivers and brooks, think that just as the waters run to the sea without ever stopping, so you too must always run to God, who is your only good. If you happen to be in a vehicle drawn by beasts of burden, say to yourself: "How these animals toil to be of service to me; and how much trouble do I take to serve and please God?" A little dog is faithful to its master for the bit of bread which it receives from him. How much more are you bound to be faithful to God, who has created you and is ever preserving you, who provides you with all goods and lavishes so many blessings on you! When you hear the singing of birds, say: "O my soul, listen to these little creatures praising their Creator. But what do *you* do?" And then make acts of love. On the other hand, when you hear the cock crow, remember that, like St. Peter, at one time you too denied your Master; and renew your sorrow and your tears. Again, when you see the house or place where you committed sin, turn to God and say: *"The sins of my youth and my ignorance do not remember."* (*Ps.* 24:7-8).

The sight of valleys made fertile by the waters running down from the mountains above should remind you that, in a similar manner, the grace of God is poured out on humble souls, but abandons the proud. When you see a beautiful church all decorated, consider the beauty of a soul in the state of grace—a real temple of God. The sea reminds us of the immensity and greatness of God. When you see a fire, or candles burning on an altar, say: "How many years I should have been burning in Hell! But since, O Lord, You have preserved me from it, grant that my heart may burn with love for You as that fire, or those candles." When you gaze at the starlit skies, say with St. Andrew Avellino: *"O my feet, one day you will tread over those stars."*

∾ Chapter 19 ∾

Conformity with the
Will of God

IN order often to call to mind the loving mysteries of our Saviour's life: when you see some hay, or a manger or a cave, think of the Infant Jesus in the stable of Bethlehem. A saw, a hammer, a plane or an axe should remind you of Jesus working like an ordinary lad in the workshop of Nazareth. Ropes, thorns, nails and wood should recall the sufferings and death of your Redeemer. The mere sight of a lamb made St. Francis of Assisi weep. *"My Lord,"* he would say, *"was led to death like a lamb for me."* Altars, chalices and patens should make you remember the great love Jesus Christ had for us in giving us the Most Blessed Sacrament.

During the day make frequent offerings of yourself to God, as St. Teresa of Avila was wont to do, by saying: "Here I am, O Lord; do with me what You please. Tell me what You wish me to do for You, and I will do it all." Repeat acts of love for God as often as you can. St. Teresa used to say that acts of love are like wood maintaining the fire of divine love kindled in our hearts.

One day the Venerable Sister Seraphina of Carpi was considering the fact that the mule of the convent was incapable of loving God, and she began to compassionate it by saying: "Poor beast, you do not know God; neither can you love Him"—and the mule acted as though it would give expression to its grief by shedding abundant tears. Thus you who can love God should be incited to make frequent acts of love when you see animals that are unable to know and love Him.

If you fall into some sin, humble yourself at once and rise again with a more fervent act of love. When something you do not want happens to you, offer it to God immediately by an act of conformity with His holy Will, and acquire the habit of always repeating in all adverse situations the words: "Such is God's Will and such also is mine." Acts of resignation are acts of love most dear and pleasing to the Heart of God.

∽ Chapter 20 ∽

Ask and You Shall Receive

WHEN you have to make a decision or give some advice on matters of importance, first of all recommend yourself to God, and then set to work or give your answer. Repeat as often as you can during the day the invocation: *"O Lord, make haste to help me."* (*Ps.* 69:2). Such was the prayer of St. Rose of Lima: *"Help me, O Lord; do not leave me in my own hands."* And therefore often look at the crucifix and at the picture of the Blessed Virgin which you have in your room, and often invoke the Holy Names of Jesus and Mary, but particularly when you are tempted.

God, because He is infinite goodness, has a great desire to grant His graces to us. The Venerable Alvarez one day saw our Saviour with His hands full of graces, going about seeking to whom He might dispense them. He wishes, however, that we ask Him for them: *"Ask and you shall receive."* (*John* 16:24). Otherwise, He withdraws His hand. But He willingly opens it to those who pray to Him. And who has ever called upon God, says Sirach, and gone away unanswered? *"Who hath called upon Him, and He despised him?"* (*Ecclus.* 2:12). David has written that the Lord is not only merciful, but exceedingly merciful, to those who pray to Him: *"For Thou, O Lord, art sweet and mild: and plenteous in mercy to all that call upon Thee."* (*Ps.* 85:5).

Oh, how good and bountiful is the Lord to those who seek Him with love! *"The Lord is good to them that hope in Him, to the soul that seeketh Him."* (*Lam.* 3:25). If He lets even those who do not seek Him find Him—*"I was found by them that did not seek Me"* (*Rom.* 10:20)— how much more readily will He be found by one who seeks Him, and who seeks Him just to serve Him and to love Him?

Finally, St. Teresa of Avila says: "Just souls upon earth must unite and conform themselves in love to that which the souls of the Blessed do in Heaven." Just as the Saints in Heaven are concerned with God alone and have no other thought and pleasure than that of His glory and of His love, so must you also. On this earth God should be your only happiness, the only object of your affections, the only purpose of all your actions and desires— so that you may arrive at the eternal kingdom where your love will be entirely perfect and full, and where your desires will be completely fulfilled and satisfied.

Live Jesus our love and Mary our hope!

SHORT PRAYERS
AND
ASPIRATIONS

To the Most Holy Trinity

To the King of ages, immortal and invisible, the only God, be honor and glory forever and ever. Amen.

Holy, Holy, Holy, Lord God of Hosts: the heavens and the earth are full of Thy glory.

With all our heart and voice, we acknowledge, we praise and we bless Thee, God the Father unbegotten; Thou the only-begotten Son; Thou, the Holy Spirit, the Paraclete: O holy and undivided Trinity!

May the most just, the most high and the most lovable Will of God be in all things done, praised, and ever more exalted. Amen.

My God and my All!

My God, grant that I may love Thee, and let the only reward of my love be to love Thee more and more. Amen.

My God, my only Good, Thou art all mine; may I be always Thine.

My God, I give You thanks for what You give, and for what You take away; Your will be done.

My God, make us to be of one mind in the truth, and of one heart in charity.

Teach me, O Lord, to do Thy Will, for Thou art my God.

O Most Holy Trinity, I adore Thee, who art dwelling by Thy grace within my soul.

O Most Holy Trinity, Who art dwelling by Thy grace within my soul, make me love Thee more and more.

O Most Holy Trinity, Who art dwelling by Thy grace within my soul, sanctify me more and more.

Abide with me, O Lord; be my true joy.

Blessed be the Name of the Lord!

My God, pour forth Thy blessings and Thy mercies upon all persons and upon all souls in Purgatory for whom, by reason of charity, gratitude and friendship, I am bound or desire to pray. Amen.

O God, be merciful to me, a sinner.

O God, Thou art all-powerful; make me a saint.   St. Alphonsus M. de Liguori

Holy God, Holy Strong One, Holy Immortal One, have mercy on us.

To Thee be praise, to Thee be glory, to Thee be thanksgiving through endless ages, O Blessed Trinity.

Blessing and glory and wisdom and thanksgiving, honor, might and power be unto our God forever and ever. Amen.

Keep me, O Lord, as the apple of Your eye; beneath the shadow of Your wings protect me.

Into Thy hands, O Lord, I commend my spirit.

O God, come to my assistance; O Lord, make haste to help me.

Vouchsafe, O Lord, this day (*or this night*) to keep us free from sin.

Deliver me, O Lord, from my enemies.

O Lord, reward us not according to the sins which we have done, nor requite us according to our iniquities.

O Lord, remember not our former iniquities, and be merciful to our sins for Thy Name's sake.

O praise the Lord, all you nations: praise Him, all you peoples.
For His mercy is confirmed upon us: and the truth of the Lord remains forever.

Holy Trinity, one God, have mercy on us!

From all sin deliver me, O Lord.

O Lord, I fear Thy justice, I implore Thy mercy. Deliver me not to everlasting pains, but grant that I may possess Thee in the midst of everlasting joys. Amen.

All through Thee, with Thee, and in Thee, O my God!

Most Holy Trinity, we adore Thee, and through Mary we implore Thee. Give to all mankind unity in the Catholic Faith and courage faithfully to confess it.

Lord, save us, we perish!

Thy will be done!

O merciful Lord, You are never weary of speaking to my poor heart; grant me the grace that, if today I hear Your voice, my heart may not be hardened.

CARDINAL MERRY DEL VAL

O Lord, I am nothing, but although nothing, I adore Thee.

CARDINAL MERRY DEL VAL

O Lord, I am my own enemy when I seek my peace apart from Thee.

CARDINAL MERRY DEL VAL

Various Acts of Faith, Hope, Charity and Contrition

My God, I believe in Thee, I hope in Thee, I love Thee above all things with all my soul, with all my heart, and with all my strength. I love Thee because Thou art infinitely good and worthy of being loved; and because I love Thee, I repent with all my heart of having offended Thee. Have mercy on me, a sinner. Amen.

O Lord, increase our faith!

My God, I love Thee.

I believe in Thee, I hope in Thee, I love Thee, I adore Thee, O Blessed Trinity, one God. Have mercy on me now and at the hour of my death, and save me. Amen.

O my soul, love the Lord that loves you from all eternity!   CARD. MERRY DEL VAL

To Our Lord Jesus Christ

My Jesus, mercy!
ST. LEONARD OF PORT MAURICE

Sweetest Jesus, be not my Judge but my Saviour.   ST. JEROME EMILIANI

Jesus, my God, I love Thee above all things.

Jesus, Son of David, have mercy on me!

O my Jesus, Thou Who art very Love, enkindle in my heart that divine fire which consumes the Saints and transforms them into Thee!

Jesus Christ, Son of the living God, Light of the World, I adore Thee. For Thee I live, for Thee I die. Amen.

Jesus, for Thee I live; Jesus, for Thee I die. I am Thine in life and in death. Amen.

O Jesus, Life Eternal in the bosom of the Father, life of souls made in Thine own likeness: in the name of Thy love, reveal Thy Heart and make It known!

O Jesus, the friend of little children, bless the little children of the whole world.

Thou art the Christ, the Son of the living God!

Blessed be Jesus Christ and His most pure Mother!

Jesus, it is for love of Thee, with Thee and for Thee.

O Jesus, Son of the living God, have mercy on us!

O Jesus, Son of the Virgin Mary, have mercy on us!

O Jesus, King and center of all hearts, grant that peace may be in Thy kingdom.

O Jesus, with all my heart I cling to Thee.

O Jesus, be to me *Jesus*,* and save me.

Christ Jesus, my Helper and my Redeemer!   ST. AUGUSTINE

O Lord Jesus Christ, Thou alone art holy, Thou alone art Lord, Thou alone art the Most High, with the Holy Spirit, in the glory of God the Father. Amen.

O Jesus, grant that I may be Thine, wholly Thine, forever Thine. Amen.

> All honor, laud and glory be,
> O Jesus, Virgin-born, to Thee:
> All glory, as is ever meet,
> To Father and to Paraclete.

---

*"Be to me Jesus" means "Be my Saviour."
—*Publisher*, 2005.

Lamb of God, Who takes away the sins of the world, grant us Thy peace.

Grant to us, Thy servants, O Lord Jesus Christ, to be protected at all times and in all places by the patronage of Blessed Mary, Thy Virgin Mother. Amen.

O sweetest Jesus, hide me in Thy Sacred Heart, permit me not to be separated from Thee, defend me from the evil foe. Amen.

O Lord Jesus,
Through Your infant cries when You were born for me in the manger,
Through Your tears when You died for me on the Cross,
Through Your love as You live for me in the tabernacle,
Have mercy on me and save me!

My dearest Jesus, teach me to be patient when all the day long my heart is troubled by little but vexatious crosses. Amen.   CARDINAL MERRY DEL VAL

To the Most
Blessed Sacrament

O Jesus in the Blessed Sacrament, have mercy on us!

May praise and adoration ever more be given to the most holy Sacrament!

O Sacrament most holy, O Sacrament divine,
All praise and all thanksgiving be every moment Thine!

I adore Thee at every moment,
O living Bread from Heaven,
O Great Sacrament!

Blessed is He who comes in the name of the Lord; Hosanna in the highest!

Jesus, my God, I adore Thee here present in the Sacrament of Thy love!

To the Sacred Heart of Jesus

May the Sacred Heart of Jesus be loved in every place!

Sweet Heart of my Jesus, grant that I may ever love Thee more!

Heart of Jesus, burning with love for us, set our hearts on fire with love for Thee.

Jesus, meek and humble of heart, make our hearts like unto Thine.

Sacred Heart of Jesus, Thy kingdom come!

O Divine Heart of Jesus, convert sinners, save the dying, deliver the souls in Purgatory.

Sacred Heart of Jesus, I believe in Your love for me.

Glory, love and thanksgiving be to the Sacred Heart of Jesus!

O Heart of love, I put all my trust in Thee; for I fear all things from my own weakness, but I hope for all things from Thy goodness.

St. Margaret Mary Alacoque

Sweet Heart of Jesus, have mercy on us and on our erring brethren.

All for Thee, Most Sacred Heart of Jesus!

Sacred Heart of Jesus, may You be known, loved and imitated!

Heart of Jesus, I put my trust in Thee!